ARCO-AIRCAM AVIATION SERIES No. 7

P–40E, 51st Fighter Group, 16th Fighter Squadron, 10th Air Force, CBI. Peishihwa, China, Oct. 1942. In standard USAAF desert camouflage.

CURTISS P-40D-N WARHAWK

IN USSAF-FRENCH AND FOREIGN SERVICE

Illustrated & compiled by
Richard Ward

Text by
Christopher F. Shores

ACKNOWLEDGMENTS

Without the help of many friends this pictorial survey of the Warhawk, the first real fighter-bomber, could not have been published. My thanks to all who helped whose names are listed below in alphabetical order:

Roger F. Besecker, Peter M. Bowers, J. Cuny, d'E. C. Darby, Fred C. Dickey, Jnr., R. C. Jones, Ernest R. McDowell, Earl Reinert, Australian War Memorial (A.W.M.), Chinese Nationalist Air Force (C.N.A.F.), Establishment Cinematographique des Armees (E.C.A.), United States Air Force.

P–40L, Meknes Ecole de Chasse, French Air Force, Morocco. In standard USAAF desert camouflage.

PUBLISHED BY

Arco Publishing Company, Inc., 219 Park Avenue South, New York, N.Y. 10003

First Published by Osprey Publications Ltd. and Printed in Great Britain

Library of Congress No. 79-93929 · Library Edition SBN 668-02106-3 · Paperback Edition SBN 668-02105-5

Very nice flying shot of a P–40K, 46th Fighter Squadron, Central Instructors School, Randolph Field, Texas. (*USAF*).

P–40K of the 23rd Fighter Group, ex AVG 'Flying Tigers' high over rugged Chinese mountains. (*USAF*).

CURTISS P-40D-N WARHAWK

When a developed version of the P-40C Tomahawk with a more powerful Allison V-1710-34 engine and increased armament of four .50 in. wing-mounted machine guns was produced by Curtiss as the Hawk 87A and ordered by the British Government, the U.S. Army Air Force was not long in taking an interest, and this aircraft was ordered as the P-40D. An early requirement for a further increase in armament was swiftly met, and after 22 P-40Ds had left the line, the first P-40E with six wing guns appeared. Orders for 2,320 of this version were placed, though 1,500 of these were purchased under Lend-Lease funds for export to Britain.

Deliveries to fighter groups began during middle and late 1941, but it was quickly evident from observation of the war in Europe that the Allison engine did not offer sufficient altitude performance for a first rate fighter, and in an effort to improve performance a Rolls Royce Merlin engine was installed in the basic airframe in November 1941. This version was put into production as the P-40F, powered by a licence-built Packard Merlin V-1650-1; the aircraft also featured a lengthened rear fuselage, and of 1,311 built the majority were retained by the Army Air Force, though 100 were released to Russia and some were later supplied to the French. Due to shortages of the Packard Merlin powerplant, production of Allison-engined variants continued, 600 P-40Ks being ordered in October 1941, originally for China. The outbreak of war changed these plans, and most were retained for U.S. service. A further 700 were ordered, and deliveries commenced in August 1942, most going to units in Alaska and the Aleutians, some being supplied to Canadian squadrons in the same area. Early models of the K featured the short fuselage of the E, while later models had the longer fuselage of the F.

In 1943 700 P-40Ls were produced, this being a lightened, Merlin-engined development of the F with only four guns. Somewhat later 300 P-40F and L models were re-engined with Allison engines and known as P-40Rs, but these were used only for training purposes. The next, and final model to be produced for the U.S.A.A.F. was the P-40N. Originally designed as a lightened Allison-engined version of the aircraft, the first 400 built were, like the L, armed only with four guns. Later models reverted to the six gun armament and had an improved cockpit canopy for better rear view, and 3,242 of these were built, more than any other version. A large number were supplied to Commonwealth countries and the Soviet Union, but many also found their way into American units throughout the Far East, where they served until the end of the war.

THE P-40 IN SERVICE

The Pacific Area

When units of the Imperial Japanese Naval Air Force struck at American bases in the Pacific on 8 December 1941, P-40Es had reached three squadrons in the Philippines, but none were available on Hawaii, where Pearl Harbour bases were attacked. On Luzon in the Philippines were four squadrons of P-40s, the 17th and 21st at Nichols Field, each with 18 P-40Es, the 3rd at Iba and the 20th at Clark Field. The 3rd also had 18 P-40Es on hand, but the 20th still flew the older P-40C, these units forming the 24th Pursuit Group. One squadron of Seversky P-35s was also available, this being the 34th.

The initial Japanese assault on airfields on Luzon on 8 December caught the Americans in a whirl of rumours, with some aircraft in the air returning from patrol and others refuelling. It fell to the P-40Cs of the 20th Squadron to claim the first victories against the new enemy. The P-40Es were not far behind in seeing action as the 3rd Squadron, returning to Iba from patrol, were caught in the landing circuit. They managed to prevent a strafing attack, but 5 P-40s were shot down, and 3 chash-landed out of fuel, though Lt. Jack Donaldson managed to claim 2 enemy aircraft probably destroyed. Only 2 of the squadron's aircraft on the ground at the time of the attack survived, and the remaining aircraft were divided between the 17th and 21st Squadrons.

On 10th aircraft of the 17th Squadron accompanied a force attacking the Japanese invasion fleet which was approaching, and strafed various ships. Later in the day the squadron, with the 21st and 34th, took off to intercept an incoming raid. The fighters were overwhelmed by the escorts and could not disrupt the attack to any extent. After this, the surviving fighters were ordered to be retained for reconnaissance missions though this routine was broken on 16 December when Lt. Ray Wagner led two other P-40s to dive-bomb aircraft on Vigan airfield. One P-40 was shot down by ground fire, but Wagner dropped six fragmentation bombs and strafed 20 aircraft on the runway. Three days earlier on a reconnaissance over Aparri this same pilot had shot down 4 Nakajima Ki 27 'Nates' over the airfield, and strafed others.

The second P–40F of the first batch of 96 aircraft, nice flying shot. (*USAF*).

The last strike made by the fighters on Luzon was against landings being made on the north coast, the survivors then being ordered to evacuate their bases and fly to Bataan. From here several strafing attacks were made on enemy forces, and on one occasion 14 aircraft were destroyed on the ground. On 2 March 1942 the last 4 airworthy aircraft took off with 500 lb. bombs to attack shipping in Subic Bay; one P-40 was shot down and the other 3 crashed on landing, due to damage, although one transport had been sunk. No further missions could be flown.

In the meantime 18 P-40's had been delivered to Brisbane in Australia as early as 22 December 1941. These were flown to the north, and a new squadron, the 17th (Provisional), was activated on 10 January 1942, manned by survivors of the Philippines fighting and by the most experienced pilots of the newly arrived 49th Fighter Group and 35th Fighter Group, the latter being a P-39 unit. This new squadron then flew forward to the Dutch East Indies, to join British and Dutch units in the defence of Java, being based at Blimbing, near Djombang. On the squadron's first operational mission, the interception of raiders, 2 enemy aircraft were shot down for the loss of 1 P-40. A second provisional squadron, the 20th (Provisional), was formed on 20 January as soon as sufficient pilots and aircraft were available, and this was followed by the 3rd (Provisional) a few days later.

On 4 February 20th (Provisional) began flying to Java, a formation of 12 P-40s landing at Bali to refuel. 7 were pushed back into the air the moment they were refuelled, and almost immediately 20 Japanese aircraft appeared. 3 more P-40s scrambled and all were engaged, 3 victories being claimed, but 2 P-40s were shot down, 2 crash-landed, and others were destroyed on the ground. 4 aircraft flew on to Java where they were joined two days later by 6 more from a formation of 8. On 9th 9 aircraft of the 3rd (Provisional) Squadron got as far as Timor, but were unable to land due to thick cloud, and all crashed while attempting forced landings. The squadron's other 9 aircraft arrived in Java on 11th and all remaining aircraft of the three units were consolidated in the 17th Squadron.

On 17 February the Japanese landed on Bali, and this squadron intercepted 9 unescorted bombers, claiming 4 destroyed and 5 probables for the loss of 1 P-40. Two days later they broke up a bomber formation over Malang, claiming 4 escorting fighters for the loss of 3 P-40s.

Meanwhile, in Australia the 33rd Squadron was formed and moved to Darwin on 15 February for the defence of the North-Western Territories, but on 19th they were just landing from patrol when the first strike from a Japanese carrier force arrived overhead. The P-40s took off again, but 9 were shot down, the commanding officer and 3 other pilots being killed. 2 more were destroyed on the ground and only 1 aircraft landed, in a damaged condition. It is not known how many Japanese aircraft were shot down, but their second strike later in the day was unopposed.

On Java the 17th Squadron made a strike on the Bali landings on 20th, 16 P-40s escorting A-24s to the area. 2 of the fighters were shot down and 2 crashed, having run out of fuel, but 3 Japanese fighters were shot down and 1 was destroyed on the ground. In Australia 32 P-40s were loaded aboard the old aircraft carrier U.S.S. 'Langley' at Freemantle, and set sail for Java in company with the freighter 'Sea Witch', carrying 27 more in crates. Three vessels carrying a further 10 P-40s were ordered to sail to Burma instead of Java. 'Langley' was found by Japanese naval aircraft, attacked and sunk, but 'Sea Witch' arrived safely. However, the position was now desperate, and although the crated aircraft were landed, there was no time to assemble them, and those that were not pushed into the harbour, fell into Japanese hands.

During the period 21-26 February the pilots of the 17th Squadron claimed 10 enemy aircraft for the loss of 3 of their number, but by the latter date only 13 P-40s remained fit to fly. On the night of 18th Japanese forces landed on North Java and next morning 9 P-40s, 6 Hurricanes and 4 Buffalos, virtually the whole of the remaining Allied fighter strength, were thrown against the invasion fleet. 3 P-40s were lost and all the rest damaged during the attack; while refuelling in preparation for a second strike, Japanese fighters suddenly swept over Ngoro field destroying all remaining P-40s, among other aircraft, and that was the end of U.S. fighter operations in the East Indies.

Early in February the first new P-40 group, the 49th, finished arriving in Australia, and following the virtually unopposed early Japanese raids on the Darwin area, a flight of this Group was moved to Horn Island early in March. On 14th these aircraft surprised and shot down 5 raiders. Two days later an advanced echelon moved their P-40s to Darwin and this was followed by the Group's 9th Squadron. Between 28 March and 27 April 7 of 9 incoming raids were intercepted, 17 bombers and 11 fighters being claimed, 2 bombers to A.A. and the rest to the P-40s, with 6 more probably destroyed. 8 P-40s were lost and 1 damaged, but only 3 pilots were killed. 4 raids followed in June, the largest being met by 28 P-40s, and by the end of the month 13 more victories had been gained for the loss of 9 more P-40s.

Following these heavy losses, the Japanese ceased raids for a period, and by 18 July the 49th Fighter Group had 80 P-40s available in the Darwin area. Raids began again on 25th, and on 30th 27 P-40s shot down 6 Mitsubishi A6M Zero-Sens and 2 bombers, with 6 more probables for the loss of 1 P-40. This again brought a lull in the raids, but late in August they began once more. On 23rd 27 bombers with approximately 20 escorting Zeros attacked Hughes airfield, and were engaged by 18 P-40s, which gained their greatest success to date, claiming 8 fighters and 4 bombers. Shortly after this the 49th moved forward to airfields in New Guinea, and by late November the 9th Squadron had begun re-equipping with P-38s, although the 7th and 35th Squadrons were to retain their P-40s for many more months.

In May 1942 the 68th Fighter Squadron had been posted to garrison Canton in New Caledonia with 25 P-40Es, and in early 1942 the area around Australia was divided into two zones, the South Pacific and the South-West Pacific. In the former, the 13th U.S. Air Force was to operate, and initially this organisation had only one P-40 Squadron, the 68th, on strength. The 5th Air

P–40E, 20th Pursuit Group (Interceptor), 79th Fighter Squadron, Hamilton Field, California, in the markings of the 1941 War Games. The War Games marking consisted of a large crude white cross on each side of the fuselage and inboard of national insignia on upper and under surfaces of the wings. (*Peter M. Bowers*).

P–40E, 20th PG(I), 79th FS, War Games 1941, large white circles in same positions as crosses. (*Peter M. Bowers*).

Line-up of 20th Pursuit Group P–40E's, note position of white cross varied considerably. (*Peter M. Bowers*).

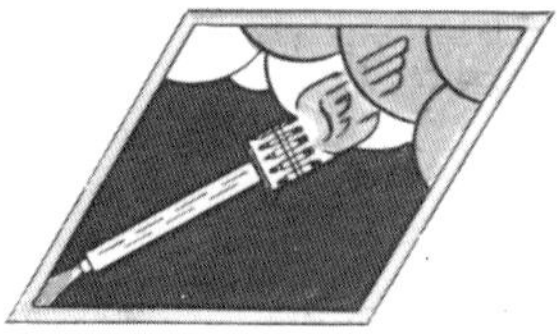

11th Fighter Squadron.

Force was to operate in the S.W.P.A., and this included the 49th F.G. on its inventory, the 8th F.G. also operating some of these aircraft alongside their P-39s.

P-40s with the 5th Air Force

From their new base in New Guinea, the pilots of the 49th F.G. continued their run of successes during the Bismark Sea operations in January 1943. On 8th they dive-bombed transport ships with 300 lb. bombs as the Japanese tried to build up their garrison on the north coast of the island, and also shot down 28 defending aircraft. On 6 February 8 P-40s from the Group intercepted 12 Kawasaki Ki 88 'Lily' bombers and 12 escorts, claiming 7 shot down. The following month the 43 P-40s and 18 P-38s of the Group began moving forward again from Port Moresby to Dobodura, and fought several more heavy engagements with the enemy during the next two months, inflicting substantial losses.

The opportunities for P-40s to take part in air combat became less during the summer of 1943 with the advent of more modern, longer-ranging aircraft, and the reduction in Japanese aerial resistance, and operations veered more and more towards ground support. By August 1943 the 5th Air Force still had 118 P-40s on strength but many of these were now in depots. However, on occasions the older fighters were still able to show their teeth, as on 2 January 1944, during the landings on Saidor; over Oro Bay 9 Mitsubishi 'Helens' escorted by 20 'Zekes' and 'Tonys' appeared and were intercepted by 12 patrolling P-40s of the 49th's 7th Squadron, 2 Helens and 3 fighters being claimed for the loss of 1 P-40.

In May the two P-40 Squadrons moved to Hollandia, and on 7th escorted heavy bombers to Mokmer, claiming 8 attacking fighters. Eight days later, while escorting a reconnaissance F-7 over Biak, pilots of the 7th Squadron claimed a further 7 Japanese fighters. These were the final victories for the P-40s in the New Guinea area.

By the time the invasion of the Philippines in late 1944 the 49th F.G. had fully re-equipped wih P-38s, but by this time the 82nd and 110th Reconnaissance Squadrons had replaced P-39s with P-40Ns which they operated for a short period before P-51s became available. On 24 December the 110th Rcc. Squadron took part, with other aircraft, in a strike on a Japanese naval unit. Losses during this attack were heavy, 6 of 20 P-40Ns taking part being lost, several on the long return flight. By early 1945 the P-40 had been phased out of service entirely with front-line echelons of the 5th Air Force.

P-40s with the 13th Air Force in the South Pacific

Apart from one squadron on garrison duty, no P-40 units served with the 13th Air Force until early 1943. Then, during the American build-up on Guadalcanal, the 18th Fighter Group began arriving with P-40s, the 44th Squadron in particular operating this fighter with considerable success, claiming 57 victories for the loss of

Early P-40N showing leading/trailing edge dapple camouflage in medium green. (*USAF*).

3 aircraft between 19 January and 1 July 1943 while undertaking interceptions, escorts, dive-bombing and strafing attacks. During June a number of large Japanese sweeps were made against the island, and on 12th 18 P-40s and some Marine F4Fs in company with R.N.Z.A.F. Kittyhawks, intercepted a large raid by 50 'Vals' and 66 'Zekes', the P-40s claiming 20 aircraft, half of them fighters, for the loss of 1 aircraft which collided with an F4F. The New Zealanders claimed 6 more for 1 loss, and the F4Fs 30, for the loss of 4.

On 4 August the P-40s were again successful, 10 of them claiming 8 'Zekes', 4 alone being credited to Lt. L. B. Shuler, but shortly after this the Group began receiving their first P-38s, which steadily replaced the P-40s, until by the late summer of 1944 all had gone, the Group having operated the E, F, M and N models. The top 'ace' of the 13th Air Force, Capt. Robert R. Westbrook, served with the 18th Group, claiming his first 7 victories on the P-40.

P-40s with the 10th and 14th Air Forces in the China-Burma-India Theatre

When the Japanese attacked Burma in December 1941 the British defenders were assisted by squadrons of the Tomahawk-equipped American Volunteer Group, which was then part of the Chinese Air Force. It was immediately planned to incorporate this unit within the U.S.A.A.F., and a shipment of P-40Es were sent to Takoradi, in West Africa, to be ferried in by air. The first few to arrive went to Burma, but the majority, arriving in May and June, went direct to China, where in the latter month the A.V.G. became the 23rd Fighter Group of the U.S.A.A.F.

As already mentioned, ships carrying 10 P-40s for Java had been re-routed to Burma, and these with the ground echelon of the 51st Fighter Group, began forming in India, the 16th Squadron being ready for operations by the end of June, and joined the 3 squadrons of the 23rd F.G., the 74th, 75th and 76th in China in what was to become the 14th Air Force. During July these squadrons shot down 24 fighters and 12 bombers for the loss of 5 P-40s. Leading the Group at the time was Lt.-Col. Robert L. Scott, who had been attached for a short while to the A.V.G. before taking command of the 23rd and who became top ranking U.S.A.A.F. 'ace' of the time with 13 victories by December 1942 in P-40s.

In India the nucleus of the 10th Air Force was formed to operate in Burma and protect the air route through Assam and over the Himalayas. The two other squadrons of the 51st F.G., the 25th and 26th, were based in the Calcutta area in 1942, but in October were rushed to Assam and took part in many attacks on railways and other targets, experimenting with the carrying of 1,000 lb. bombs.

In summer 1943 the squadrons in China received P-40Ks and Ms, but better Japanese fighters were appearing and life for the Warhawk pilots became more difficult. On 20 August enemy fighters used the P-40s' own tactics on them, diving from altitude and shooting down 3 P-40s for the loss of 2, before climbing out of reach again. In September a new Group, the 80th, arrived at Karachi, and after exchanging a number of pilots with the 51st F.G. to give the new squadrons some experienced personnel, they took over from the two squadrons of the 51st, which flew to China to join the other two now there, the 16th and 449th, to unite the Group for the first time.

The 80th began operations with P-40Ns, and these better-climbing aircraft also began joining the units in China. Here, during the summer, the first Chinese-American Composite Wing was formed, and this included two P-40 Groups, the 3rd and 5th, being numbered within the Chinese, rather than the American Army Air Force, each being comprised of 4 squadrons. In all 377 P-40s were to be supplied to China during the war, mainly for use in these Groups. A second Composite Wing was later formed, one fighting on each of the main fronts in China, as did the two U.S. fighter groups.

Early in April 1944 the 23rd Fighter Group began re-equipping with early-model P-51s, and other American and Chinese units followed suite during 1944, the number of P-40s in use reducing month by month, from 205 in December 1944 to 62 in July 1945 when the war ended.

P-40s with the 11th Air Force in the Aleutians

In December 1941 the 25 P-40s of the 11th Fighter Squadron were ordered to the Aleutian Islands in the North Pacific, off Alaska. By late January 1942 only 13 had arrived in flyable condition, and on 23 May 10 of these moved to the island of Umnak. By 3 June 12 were available when a Japanese fleet attacked, and occupied the island of Kiska. Cruisers despatched floatplanes over Umnak in heavy cloud, but P-40s shot down one of these and damaged a second.

Aircraft from the carriers 'Ryujo' and 'Junyo' attacked the U.S. bases, but during the second strike on 4 June, 8 P-40s intercepted 4 dive-bombers and 4 fighters, shooting down 2 of each for the loss of 2 P-40s. Later in the year reinforcements arrived, including the 18th Squadron with P-40s. Although bad weather continually restricted operations, the Americans then went onto the offensive, and on 25 September 10 B-24s, a B-17, 11 P-39s and 6 P-40s, with 11 Kittyhawks of 111

Another shot showing the dapple camouflage, note wing ailerons have no dapple though it was usually applied the full trailing edge span. (*USAF*).

Squadron, R.C.A.F., also taking part in operations in the area, attacked Kiska, 2 Mitsubishi 'Rufe' fighter/float-planes being shot down, one by the Canadians, and 5-8 were destroyed on the water. Throughout early 1943 the P-40s carried out fighter-bomber attacks on Kiska, carrying a 500 lb. bomb and 6 20 lb. fragmentation bombs on each aircraft, operating now from Amchitka. By May of that year 80 P-40s were available, 23 at Amchitka, 22 at Adak and 35 at Umnak, these forming the 343rd Fighter Group, but in August the Japanese withdrew from Kiska, and no further action took place in this area.

P-40s with the 7th Air Force in the Central Pacific

After recovering from the Japanese attack on Hawaii, the 7th Air Force was formed to defend the Central Pacific area. After the battle of Midway, the 25 P-40Es of the 73rd Fighter Squadron were taken out to Midway Island on U.S.S. 'Saratoga' to relieve Marine units there, and remained until January 1943, when replaced by the 78th Squadron. By August 1942 the 7th had 200 fighters available, and by October this total had risen to 319, mainly P-40s.

During 1944 P-40Ns arrived, and equipped with these the 45th Squadron of the 15th Fighter Group took part in neutralization of several Japanese islands, including Mille and Jaliut, flying escorts and strafing and bombing in company with A-24s, P-39s, F6Fs, SBDs, B-25s and B-24s.

The Mediterranean Area

P-40s with the 9th and 12th Air Force in the Mediterranean

Following the fall of Tobruk to Rommel's Afrika Korps in June 1942, U.S.A.A.F. assistance was sent hastily to the R.A.F. in the Western Desert of North Africa. First fighter unit to arrive in Egypt was the 57th Fighter Group with P-40Fs, and the squadrons of this unit flew their first operations during August and September, initially attached to R.A.F. Kittyhawk Wings. First claims were made on 9 August when Lt. William O'Neil claimed 2 Bf 109s before he was forced to bail out into the sea. The three squadrons first operated as a Group during the Alamein battle, and on 27 October 16 P-40s from the 64th and 65th Squadrons on a bombing mission met a large formation of Ju 87s and Fiat CR 42s, claiming 7 destroyed, 3 probables and 3 damaged without loss. By the end of the battle 20 victories had been claimed, and during November 112 Squadron, R.A.F., joined the Group to operate as a pair with the 66th Squadron, remaining for about three months. By the end of January 1943 when the Group was rested, 64 victories had been claimed for the loss of 21 P-40s.

A second unit, the 79th F.G., had arrived late in 1942, and key personnel were attached to the 57th for experience during December. This new Group first went into action in March 1943, and both groups, each accompanied by one squadron of the third fighter group to arrive, the 324th, took part in the Mareth Line battle later that month.

While the units of what had become the 9th Air Force, were operating with the R.A.F. over Alamein, another P-40F group was going into action some hundreds of miles to the west. Various units had been gathered to form the U.S. 12th Air Force for the invasion of French North Africa. The 33rd Fighter Group arrived on the carrier U.S.S. 'Chenango' and flew off to land in the Casablanca area on 8 November 1942, but lost 2 aircraft with 17 more damaged trying to get into airfields around Port Lyautey. 35 more aircraft were brought in on H.M.S. 'Archer' a few days later, and the Group's 58th Squadron went into action from Thelepte, Tunisia, on 6 December, joined next day by the 60th and a little later by the 59th. The Group, as part of XII Air Support Command, provided air cover for U.S. ground forces and escorts to A-20s and P-39s. During this period Axis attacks were frequent and although victories were numerous losses were also high.

After initially opposing the Allied landings, the French became allies, and it was decided to equip one fighter unit for action. Late in December P-40Fs destined for the 33rd F.G. were given instead to GC II/5 to replace their Curtiss Hawk 75As, and this unit became the Groupe Lafayette, moving to Southern Tunisia in early January to join the 33rd F.G. En route, two N.C.O. pilots defected to the French mainland, but the rest were soon in action from Thelepte, claiming 2 Ju 88s on 10th and losing 2 P-40s in action next day.

The 33rd had claimed 15 aircraft by 13 January, as well as many tanks, vehicles etc., on the ground, and on 10th Maj. Philip Cochrane had dropped a bomb on the German H.Q. at the Hotel Splendida in Kairouan. On 15 January the unit intercepted 9 bombers over Thelepte and shot down 8, but on 22nd Rommel's offensive towards the Kasserine Pass saw the unit full-out on ground attack missions. Losses were heavy at this time, and on 3 February in three missions 9 P-40s were lost, on one occasion only 1 from a formation of 6 returning. Shortly after this, with only 13 of the original 71 aircraft left, the group withdrew to rest and re-equip, returning to operations in March, mainly in the bomber escort role. During this second tour successes far outstripped losses for this now seasoned unit, and when the Axis surrender in Tunisia occurred in mid May, one pilot, Maj. Levi Chase, was American top-scorer for the campaign, with 10 victories.

The Groupe Lafayette claimed a further 5 victories for the loss of 6 P-40s, but were forced to retreat with U.S. units in mid February from Thelepte, losing more aircraft which were abandoned. In mid March the Groupe flew to Morocco to rest and re-equip with P-40Ls. 36 of these were received, more than were needed for the two escadrilles of the groupe, so the 1st Escadrille of GC II/4 was attached. The unit flew back to Tunisia in May, too late for any more action, and remaining on patrol and defence duties in this area until the P-40s were replaced by Republic P-47s in December 1943.

The groups of the 9th Air Force, now operating in Tunisia, took part in much ground attack work, and during April patrolled the sea between Sicily and Cap Bon, looking for transports which were attempting to supply the Axis forces by air. On 18 April the three squadrons of the 57th F.G. with the 314th Squadron of the 324th F.G., 46 P-40s in all, covered by 12 Spitfires of 92 Squadron, R.A.F., flew an evening patrol, on the last leg of which they encountered an enormous formation of 90+ Ju 52s with fighter escorts, leaving the Tunisian coast. There then occurred the famous 'Palm Sunday Massacre'; it was never finalized what the total Axis losses were, but claims for 58 Ju 52s, 14 Bf 109s and 4 Bf 110s were allowed for the loss of 6 P-40s. Two pilots each shot down 5 aircraft, and one got 4 during this mission.

The 79th F.G., although flying many patrols, always just missed the transports, but during late April and early May took part in many attacks on shipping, sinking a fair number of vessels. By the end of the campaign this group had claimed 26 victories in the air and lost 24 P-40s.

The final P-40 group to arrive in North Africa was probably the most successful in combat. The 325th F.G. arrived to join the 12th Air Force in January 1943, but their P-40Fs were at first borrowed for use by the 33rd F.G. The group adopted a distinctive black and yellow chequered tail as their marking, and first entered action on 17 April, claiming 2 victories over Tunisia on 6 May. Allotted to the North-West African Strategic Air Force for bomber escort duties, the only single-engined group in this force, the group took part in attacks on the island of Decimomannu during the second half of May, claiming 6 fighters on 19th and a complete formation of 7 Me 323s together with 6 fighters on 20th.

During June many sorties were flown over the island of Pantellaria, the 57th and 79th F.G.s also attacking this target in company with bombers. The 325th claimed a further 24 fighters by 10 June, while on this latter date one squadron of the 79th claimed 15 victories over the island, Lt. Paul G. McArthur shooting down 4 of these before bailing out, the first and only 'ace' of the group. In July the 325th carried out a series of escort and dive-bombing missions against Sardinia, and continued these until late August, 7 victories being claimed on 28th. These were the last of 135 victories by this group with the P-40, all being gained in 110 missions for the loss of 32 aircraft; four pilots each gained 6 victories during this period.

In the meantime the 33rd, 57th, 79th and 324th Groups were providing cover for the Allied landings on Sicily. The 324th had finally come together as a group in May, and now patrolled the beaches, while in mid July the 57th and 79th moved to airstrips on the island. The 79th F.G. fought a couple of combats during August over Southern Italy, claiming 5 enemy fighters to bring the group score to 54, but these were to be their last of the war.

A few days later the 9th Air Force was disbanded to re-form in England, and all fighter groups were transferred to the 12th, the three P-40 groups later taking part in the invasion of Italy; they continued to fly close support missions from bases in this country for some time. In mid September 1943 the 325th F.G. handed their P-40s to the 324th and converted to P-47s. On 1 February 1944 the 33rd F.G., which had been involved mainly in shipping patrols since the end of the Tunisian campaign, was withdrawn to re-equip, and then moved to the C.B.I. theatre. The three remaining groups soldiered on in Italy with their P-40s for a few more months, but all were steadily re-equipped with P-47s. Throughout the Mediterranean fighting all groups operated mainly the Merlin-powered P-40Fs and Ls, but in Africa the 57th F.G. also had on strength a few P-40Ks.

Other Service

Apart from operational use, the Warhawk was also used to a large extent for advanced training in the U.S. and also formed the initial equipment of many fighter groups as they formed. The French also used the P-40 for training in North Africa, where the aircraft remained in service until 1946-7.

Two other air forces also operated the P-40; 89 aircraft were supplied to Brazil following that nation's declaration of war on Germany and Italy, while others served in Chile after the Chilean Air Force was re-organised under American supervision.

Fighter Units operating the P-40 Warhawk in the U.S.A.A.F.

Philippines	24th P.G.
5th Air Force	8th, 49th F.G.s
7th Air Force	15th F.G.
9th Air Force	57th, 79th, 324th F.G.s
11th Air Force	343rd F.G.
12th Air Force	33rd, 57th, 79th, 324th, 325th F.G.s
13th Air Force	18th F.G., 68th F.S.
10th/14th Air Force	23rd, 51st, 80th F.G.s

Most succesful P-40 Warhawk pilots

5th Air Force

Capt. Robert M. De Haven	10	49th F.G.
Capt. Ernest A. Harris	10	49th F.G.
Capt. Andrew J. Reynolds	10	17th (Prov.) Sqn., 49th F.G.

9th/12th Air Force

Maj. Levi Chase	10	33rd F.G.
Lt.-Col. William W. Momyer	8	33rd F.G.
Capt. Roy E. Whittaker	7	57th F.G.

13th Air Force

Capt. Lucien B. Shuler	7	18th F.G.
Capt. Robert B. Westbrook	7	18th F.G.
Capt. Elmer Wheadon	7	18th F.G.

10th/14th Air Force

Capt. John F. Hampshire	17	23rd F.G.
Col. John C. Herbst	14	23rd F.G.
Col. Bruce K. Holloway	13	23rd F.G.
Col. Robert L. Scott	13	23rd F.G.

Note: These scores are not necessarily the final totals for each of the pilots mentioned, only the victories actually claimed by them whilst flying the P-40 Warhawk range.

P–40N of the last batch built. (*USAF*).

Good detail close-up of a P–40E of the 343rd Fighter Group, 11th Fighter Squadron, 11th Air Force. Aleutians Island. Note yellow wheels discs. *(USAF)*

Line-up of 343rd FG, P–40E's, nearest Warhawk is of the 18th FS, 11th FS aircraft further down the line. Note P–39's, B–24's and C–47's dispersed round the strip. Adak Island, Aleutians. (*USAF*).

Two P–40E's of the 11th Fighter Squadron taxying out for take-off on Unmak Island, Aleutians. Nearest aircraft has 96 on fin, line-up of P–40E's in background all have the 'Bengal Tiger' marking on their noses. (*USAF*).

Above: P–40E, 343rd Fighter Group, 11th Fighter Squadron, 11th Air Force, revving up prior to take-off from Unmak strip. (*USAF*).

Right: Another P–40E of the 11th Fighter Squadron on dispersal area at Unmak, note aircraft number 63, grey wheel discs with yellow outer ring. (*USAF*).

Below: Same aircraft as shown in top photograph, note rather crude application of 'Bengal Tiger' marking. (*USAF*).

Above: P–40E, 343rd Fighter Group, 18th Fighter Squadron, 11th Air Force, Adak Island, Aleutian Islands, 1943. Note Squadron marking on rudder. (*IWM*).

Above: P–40E of the 11th Fighter Squadron being re-armed, Unmak strip. Note filled-in exhaust aperture. (*USAF*).

Below: Line-up of P–40K's of the Chinese American Çomposite Wing at either Chikian or Kunming, China, under the command of the 14th Air Force. (*CNAF/NA*).

P–40K of the Chinese American Composite Wing at either Chikian or Kunming, China. Note five Japanese flags under cockpit with pilot's name, Major Edward Hollmeyer just ahead. Insignia in Sharkmouth, see page 10. (*USAF*).

Interesting photograph showing at left a 23rd Fighter Group P–40B and to the right a P–40K, 103 on fuselage and slightly ahead the old AVG 'Flying Tigers' insignia. Note P–43 in background. *(USAF)*

Mixed formation of 23rd Fighter Group Warhawks, two P–40K's, 365 and 360 and an N, 370. Note different camouflage schemes. *(USAF)*.

Line-up of Warhawks of the 23rd Fighter Group at Chengkung Airfield, China. Note spinners are white and red, nearest aircraft 359 in white on fin, third aircraft 352. *(USAF)*.

Above: Interesting photograph taken in a maintenance unit hangar somewhere in China. Note Tomahawk with white 14 on fuselage carries the 'Flying Tiger' insignia, and also in small characters on fin a Chinese serial P–8127. (*USAF*).

Above: P–40K Warhawk of the 23rd Fighter Group, white 110 on fuselage, note two drop tanks in tandem under fuselage.

Right: Line-up of 23rd Fighter Group P–40K's outside the old hangar at Kunming airfield, China. Aircraft numbers from left to right 113, 117, 108, standard USAAF desert camouflage with US Army on under surface of wings.

Below: Line-up of P–40K's with the exception of the third aircraft which is a P–40B, 23rd Fighter Group, 14th Air Force, China. (*IWM*).

Above left: Crew Chief, J. R. Hill of Cleveland, Ohio, points to score on Colonel Robert Scott's P–40 of the 23rd Fighter Group. Two JAAF and three JNAS. See colour illustration. (*USAF*).

Above right: Colonel Robert L. Scott helps to re-arm his P–40K at Kunming, China. (*USAF*).

Above: Lt. D. D. Bryant of the 51st Fighter Group, 16th Fighter Squadron, having his P-40 re-fuelled at Peishihwa, China, October 1942. Note this is the second aircraft in the line-up at top of next page. (*USAF*).

Below: Line-up of Warhawks of the 51st Fighter Group, 16th Fighter Squadron, Peishihwa, China, October 1942.

Above: Warhawks of the 51st Fighter Group, 16th Fighter Squadron, neatly lined up at Peishihwa, China. Fourth aircraft is 'Rose Marie' flown by Lt. R. H. Mooney. (*USAF*).

Below: P–40N's probably of the 23rd Fighter Group being re-fuelled and re-armed on a Chinese airfield. (*USAF*).

Above: Close-up detail of Allison engine with an interesting line-up of aircraft in the background, to left two Vultee Vanguards and to the right Curtiss-Wright CW–21's. P–40K, 51st FG, 16th FS. (*USAF*).

Below: Engine maintenance on a P–40K of the 51st FG being undertaken during the rainy season on an airfield in China. (*USAF*).

Nice flying shot of 'Sue' of the 51st Fighter Group returning from a bombing mission over Burma. Note no blue outline to the white bars of the national insignia, and whip aerial on top of fuselage. Dapple medium green camouflage on wing leading and trailing edges and tail unit. (*USAF*).

Above: P–40K of the 51st Fighter Group, tucked away amongst bamboo trees alongside the runway at Lilibari airfield, India. March 1943. (*USAF*).

Above: P–40K with 'Sabre toothed' Sharkmouth, 51st Fighter Group, 25th or 26th Fighter Squadron, taking off on a bombing mission from Dinjan airfield, India. (*USN*).

Left: Two P–40K's with standard and 'Sabre toothed' Sharkmouths of the 51st Fighter Group, Dinjan airfield, India. (*USN*).

Left: P–40K on an airfield in India, note ATC insignia on fuselage side, 246 in black on fin. (*Peter M. Bowers*).

Japs and Mustangs were all the same to the Warhawk or so it would seem from this photograph, result of a taxying accident during an air-raid alarm on a Chinese airfield. 51st Fighter Group. (*USAF*).

Above: Early P–40N of the 80th Fighter Group, 85th Fighter Squadron, 10th Air Force, CBI, taking off from the jungle airstrip at Tingwak Sakan, Burma, 1943. Both aircraft with medium green dapple camouflage.

Above & right: Line-up of P–40N's of the 80th Fighter Group, 85th Fighter Squadron at Nagahuli airfield, Assam, India May 1944. (*USAF*)

Right: Nose detail of P–40N flown by Col. Ivan W. McElroy, OC 80th Fighter Group. (*USAF via R. C. Jones*).

Above: Low level beat-up by Warhawks of the 49th Fighter Group, 7th Fighter Squadron at Dobodura Fighter Strip, New Guinea. (*Australian War Memorial*).

Above: Line-up of same four P–40's as in the above photograph, third aircraft with 'Sharkmouth' evidently a member of Capt. Nick Nichol's 'Nip Nippers'. (*AWM*).

Right: P–40N of the 49th Fighter Group, probably 7th Fighter Squadron New Guinea. See colour illustration. (*Frank F. Smith*).

Line-up of P–40N's of the 49th Fighter Group, 7th Fighter Squadron, 5th Air Force, SWPA. On the airstrip at Cape Gloucester, New Britain, June, 1944. See colour illustration. (*USAF*).

P–40N, 18th Fighter Group, 44th Fighter Squadron, 7th Air Force, POA, coming in to land at Munda airfield, New Georgia Island, Solomon Islands, shortly after the field was captured by American forces. (*USAF*).

1
P–40E, 20th Pursuit Group (Interceptor), 79th Pursuit Squadron, Hamilton Field, California, 1941.

2
P–40E, 343rd Fighter Group, 11th Fighter Squadron, 11th Air Force, Elmendorf Field, Alaska, 1942. Aleutian Islands Campaign.

3
P–40E, 343rd Fighter Group, 11th Fighter Squadron, 11th Air Force, Adak Island, Aleutian Islands, 1943.

4
P–40E, 343rd Fighter Group, 18th Fighter Squadron, 11th Air Force, Adak Island, Aleutian Island, 1943.

5
P–40K, 46th Fighter Squadron, Central Instructors School, 1943.

6
P–40K, Chinese American Composite Wing, Chikian, China. Under command of 14th Air Force.

© WARRD—

B

1
P–40K, 23rd Fighter Group, The 'Flying Tigers', Kunming, China, 1942. 14th Air Force, CBI.

2
P–40K, 23rd Fighter Group, Kunming, China, 1942. 14th Air Force, CBI.

3
P–40E, 23rd Fighter Group, flown by Col. Robert L. Scott, Group Commander. Mid 1942.

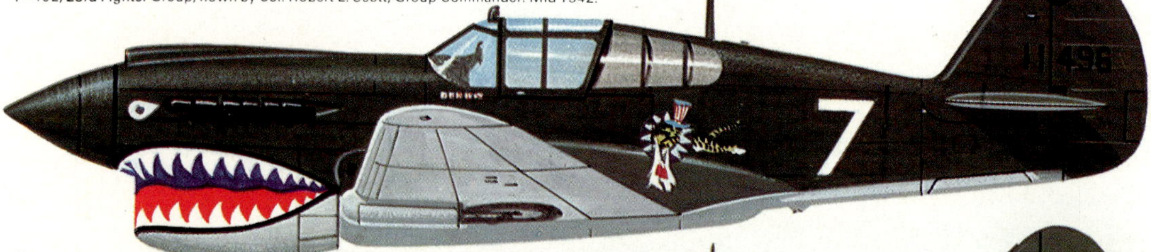

4
P–40K, 23rd Fighter Group, flown by Col. Robert L. Scott, Group Commander, Late 1942.

5
P–40K, 23rd Fighter Group 68th Composite Wing, Liuchow, China, 1943. 14th Air Force, CBI.

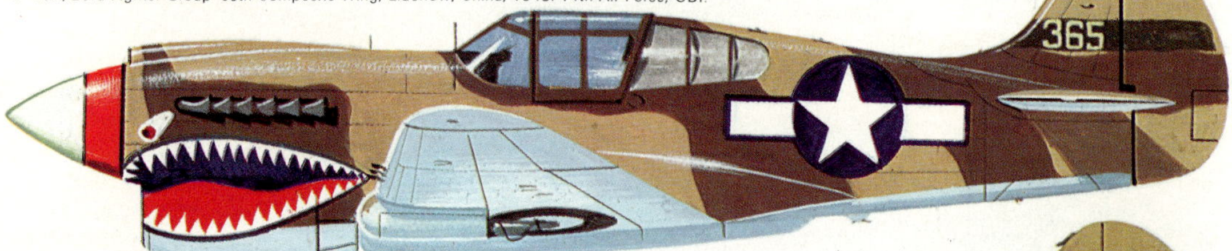

6
P–40K, 51st Fighter Group, 25th or 26th Fighter Squadron, 10th Air Force, CBI. Dinjan, India.

ARCO-AIRCAM AVIATION SERIES

UNIT INSIGNIA

AERONAVALE

UI/No. 7

CIRCA 1945-1968

Escadrille 1F (later 11F)

Seafire Mk III, XV
Grumman F6F-5 Hellcat
Aquilon, Etendard IVM

Escadrille 3F

Curtiss SB2C-5 Helldiver

Escadrille 4F

Douglas SBD-5 Dauntless
Curtiss SB2C-5 Helldiver
Grumman TBM-3 Avenger
Alize

Escadrille 6F

Lockheed Ventura
MB 175T
Grumman TBM-3 Avenger
Alize

Escadrille 7F

Short Sunderland

Escadrille 8F

Consolidated PBY-5 Catalina,
Consolidated PB4Y-4 Privateer

Escadrille 9F

Grumman TBM-3 Avenger
Alize

Escadrille 12F

Grumman F6F-5 Hellcat
Vought F4U-7 & AU-1 Corsair

Escadrille 14F

Vought F4U-7 & AU-1 Corsair
Vought F8U-FN Crusader

Escadrille 15F

Vought F4U-7 Corsair
Etendard IVM

Escadrille 16F

Aquilon

Escadrille 17F

Aquilon
Etendard IVM

Escadrille 22F

Breguet Atlantic

Escadrille 10S

MB 175T, Junkers Ju.52
Avro Lancaster, SNJ-, SB2C-,
TBM-3, SO 95.

Escadrille 53S

Dornier Do. 24
Supermarine Walrus
Martinet

Escadrille 54S (Training Unit)

Grumman F6F-5 & 5N Hellcat
Aquilon

Escadrille 56S

Bell 47
Alouette II & III

Escadrille 59S

Aquilon
Fouga Zephyr
Etendard IVM & IVP

Aeronavale Base Hyeres

Aeronavale Base Istres

Published by ARCO PUBLISHING COMPANY, INC., 219 Park Avenue South, N.Y., N.Y. 10003. Printed in Great Britain.

C

1
P–40N, 80th Fighter Group, 85th Fighter Squadron, 10th Air Force, CBI. Tingwak Sakan, Burma, 1943.

2
P–40N/5, 80th Fighter Group, 85th Fighter Squadron, 10th Air Force, CBI, Nagahuli, Assam, India, 1944.

3
P–40N/5, 80th Fighter Group, 85th Fighter Squadron, 10th Air Force, CBI, Nagahuli, Assam, India, 1944.

4
P–40N 49th Fighter Group, 7th Fighter Squadron, 5th Air Force, SWPA, Gusap, New Guinea, 1943.

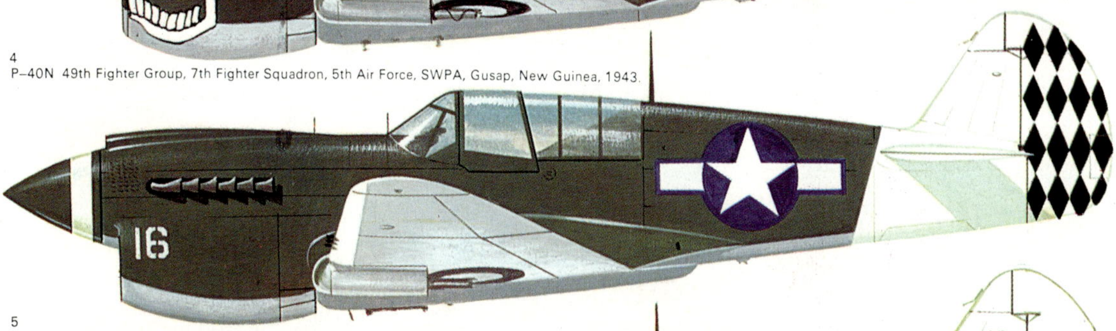

5
P–40N/5, 49th Fighter Group, 7th Fighter Squadron, 5th Air Force, SWPA. Cape Gloucester, New Britain, June 1944.

6
P–40N/20, USAAF/RAAF Pool aircraft, New Guinea. USAAF serial 363187, RAAF A29–369.

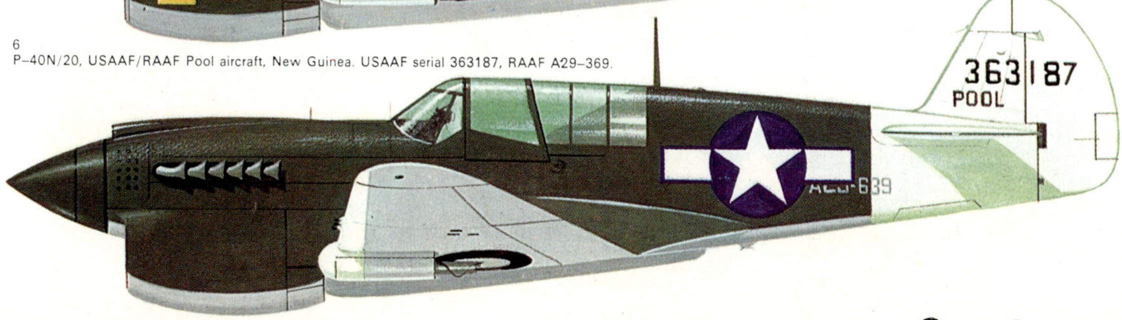

© WARRD—

D

1
P–40K, 57th Fighter Group, 64th Fighter Squadron, 9th Air Force, Western Desert, 1943.

2
P–40F/10, 57th Fighter Group, 64th Fighter Squadron, 9th Air Force, Western Desert, 1943.

3
P–40F, 57th Fighter Group, 65th Fighter Squadron, 9th Air Force. Under command of No. 211 Group, Desert Air Force, RAF.

4
P–40F/1, 57th Fighter Group, 65th Fighter Squadron, 9th Air Force. Western Desert, 1943. 'Grim Rip'

5
P–40F, 57th Fighter Group, 65th Fighter Squadron, 9th Air Force. Western Desert, 1943.

6
P–40F, 57th Fighter Group, 65th Fighter Squadron, 9th Air Force, Burg-el-Arab, Egypt, 1942. 'Sally'

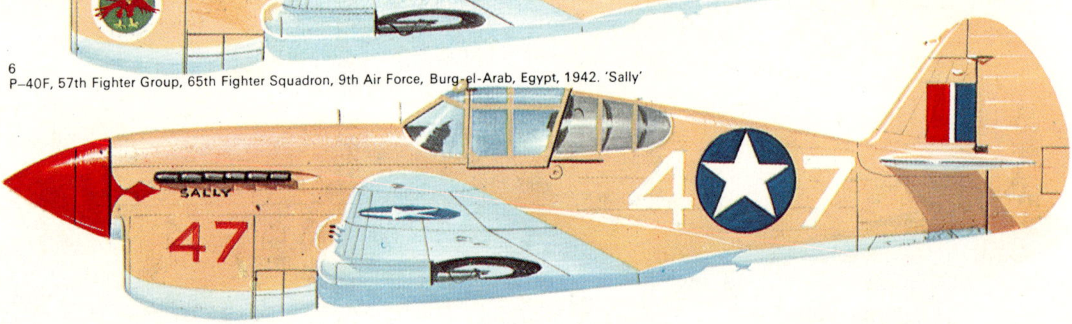

E

1
P–40F, 57th Fighter Group, 66th Fighter Squadron, 9th Air Force, Western Desert, 1942–3.

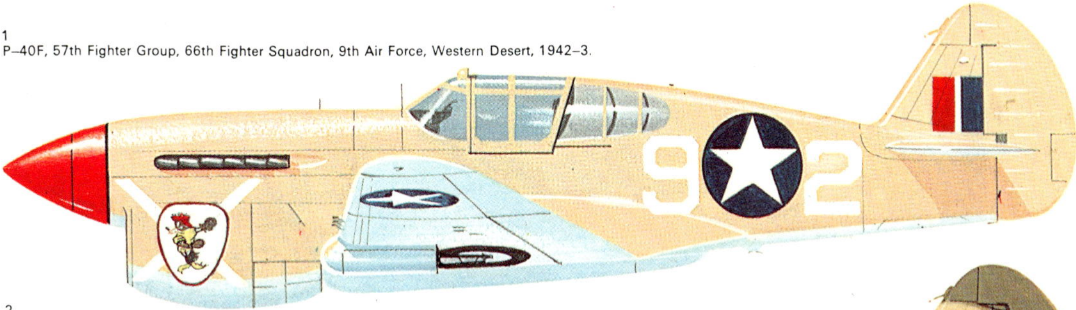

2
P–40F/1, 79th Fighter Group, 86th Fighter Squadron, 9th Air Force, Western Desert, 1943.

3
P–40F/5, 33rd Fighter Group, 12th Air Force. Operation 'Torch' North Africa. Port Lyautey, French Morocco, Nov. 1942.

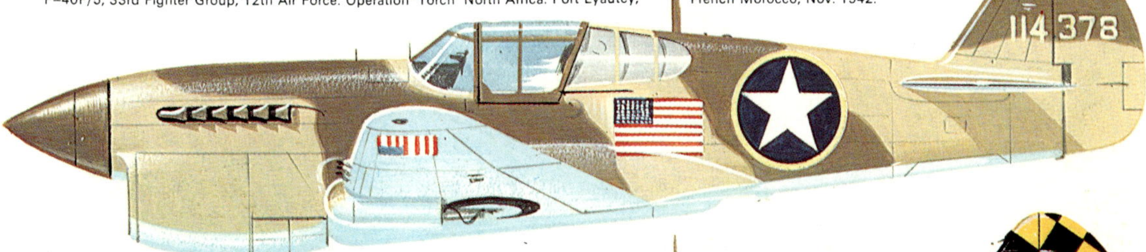

4
P–40F, 325th Fighter Group, 317th Fighter Squadron, 12th Air Force, Souk-el-Khemis, Tunisia, 1943 'Duchess of Durham'.

5
P–40F, 325th Fighter Group, 319th Fighter Squadron, 12th Air Force, Soliman, Tunisia, 1943.

6
P–40F, Unit unknown, Italy.

© WARRD

F

1
P–40N, 18th Fighter Group, 44th Fighter Squadron, 7th Air Force, POA. Munda Field, New Georgia, Soloman Islands. Aug. 1943.

2
P–40N/5, 15th Fighter Group, 45th Fighter Squadron, 7th Air Force, POA. Nanumea Island, Ellice Islands, Dec. 1943.

3
P–40L, Training unit, ZI.

4
P–40K/20, AAF Tactical Center, Orlando Field, Florida, ZI.

5
P–40N/20, AAF Tactical Center, Orlando Field, Florida, ZI.

6
TP–40M, AAF Tactical Center, Orlando, Florida, ZI. 'Short Snorter'.

©WARRD

1
TP–40N/30, Training unit, ZI. H–80 under port wing only.

2
P–40N/30, flown by Major B. Preston, OC of the 13th Pursuit Group.

3
P–40N/25, 369th Fighter Group, 398th Fighter Squadron, Hamilton Field, California, 1944.

4
P–40N, Chinese Nationalist Air Force, modified as 2 seater. Kangwan Field, 1946.

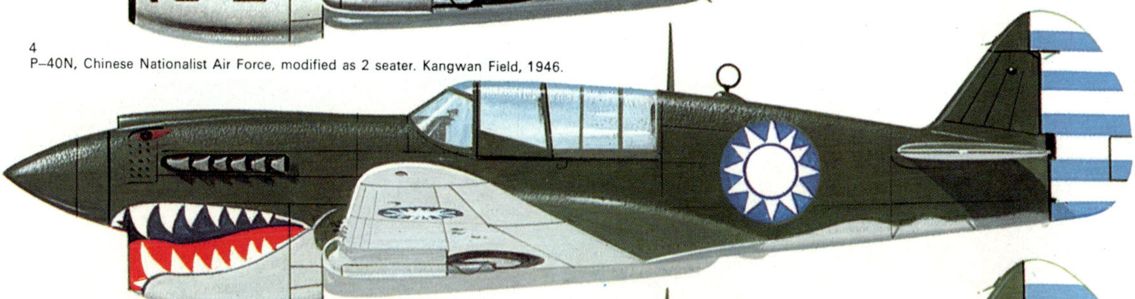

5
P–40N, Chinese Nationalist Air Force, Kangwan Field, 1946.

6
P–40M/5, Brazilian Air Force.

© WARRD —

1
P–40F/5, Groupe Lafayette flown by Commandant Rozanoff, Groupe Commander. Tunisia 1943. French Air Force. 'Madkot'.

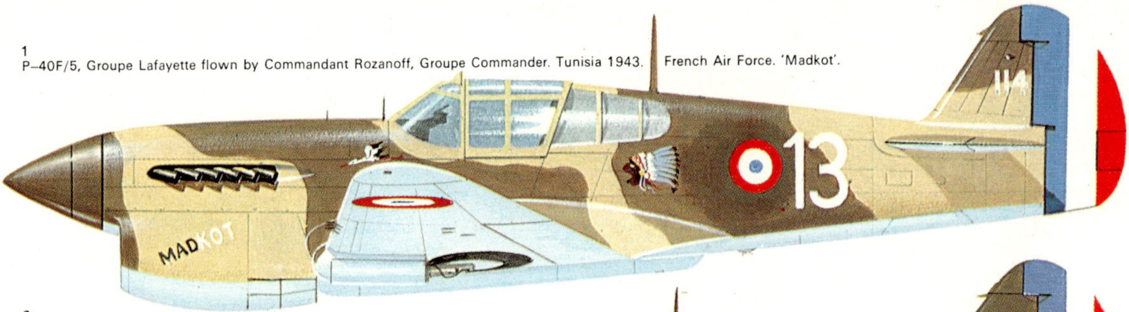

2
P–40F/1, 1st Escadrille, Groupe Lafayette, French Air Force, Tunisia, 1943.

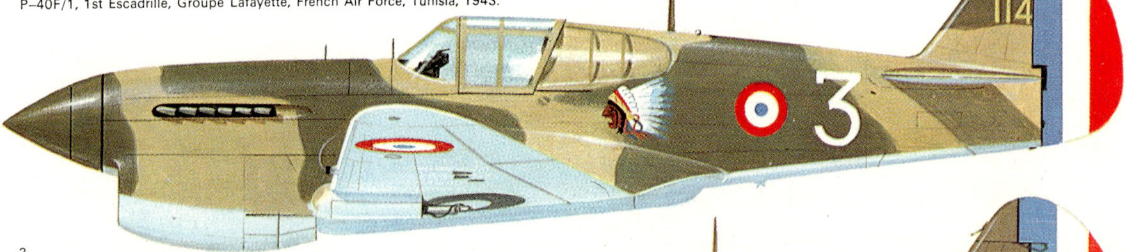

3
P–40F/1, 2nd Escadrille, Groupe Lafayette, French Air Force, Tunisia, 1943.

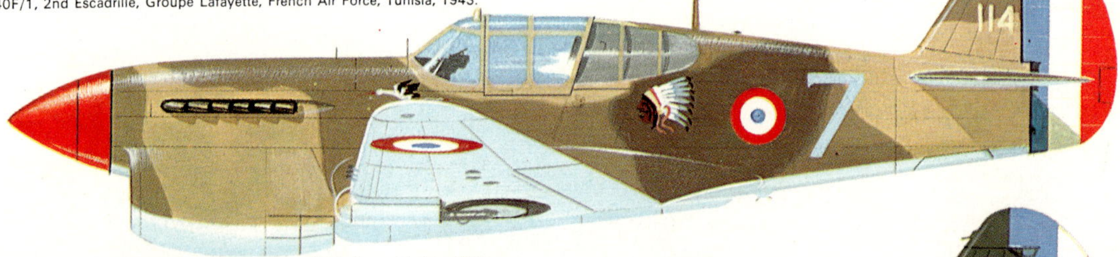

4
P–40L/10, 3rd Escadrille, Groupe Lafayette, French Air Force, Tunisia, 1943.

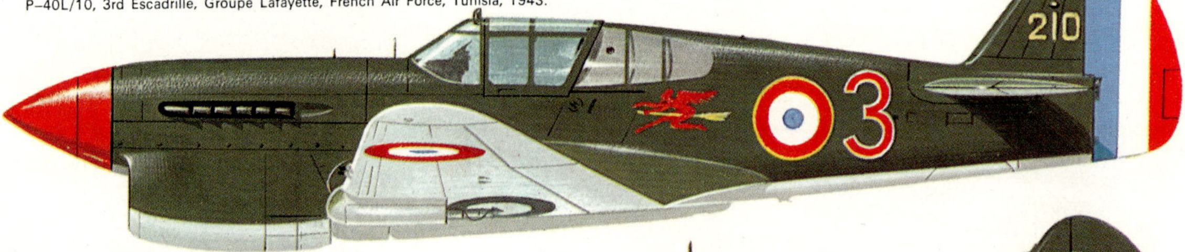

5
P–40F/5, Meknes Fighter School, French Air Force, Morocco, 1943.

6
P–40L/10, Meknes Fighter School, French Air Force, Morocco, 1943–4.

© WARD

P–40N taxying alongside the runway prior to taking off on a strafing mission at Munda airfield, Solomon Islands, August 1945. (*USAF*).

Above & below: P–40N 'Princess Pat II' being re-fuelled at Munda airfield. Note non-standard drop tank. 18th FG 44th FS. (*USAF*).

Above left: The first P–40N of the 15th FG, 45th FS, 7th AF lands on Baker Island with a second plane following it in. 11th September, 1943.
Above right: Second P–40N about to touch down on Baker Island airfield. (*Both photos USAF*).

Above & below: Line-up of P–40N's of the 15th Fighter Group, 45th Fighter Squadron, 7th Air Force, POA on Baker Island. B–24's, acting as navigators, escorted the Warhawks from Canton Island in the Phoenix Island Group. Note the cloud of coral dust behind the two aircraft taxying down the runway. (*Both Photos USAF*).

Above & below: Overall pink P–40N's of the 15th Fighter Group, 45th Fighter Squadron being re-armed on Nanumea Island, Ellice Islands. December 1943. 'Geronimo', in red with black outline serial 2105112. Note exhaust port plates. (*USAF*).

Above: P–40K of the 57th Fighter Group, 64th Fighter Squadron, 9th Air Force on a Tunisian airfield in 1943. (*USAF*).

Left: P–40F, 57th Fighter Group, 64th Fighter Squadron, 9th AF, Western Desert 1943. See colour illustration. (*via Ernest R. McDowell*).

Above: P–40F, 57th Fighter Group, 65th Fighter Squadron, crash landed in Tunisia. Note yellow surround to national insignia. (*via Frank F. Smith*).

Right: Poor photograph of a P–40F of the 57th Fighter Group, 65th Fighter Squadron, Burg-el-Arab, Egypt. Serial 113921.

Below: P–-40F downed in the desert belonging to the 57th Fighter Group, 66th Fighter Squadron, 9th Air Force. (*via E. R. McDowell*).

P–40F of the 79th Fighter Group, 86th Fighter Squadron, 9th Air Force on a desert airfield. Serial 114216. (*via Frank F. Smith*).

P–40L 'Empress' of the 79th Fighter Group, 86th Fighter Squadron, 9th Air Force. Serial 210598. (*via E. R. McDowell*).

Right: 'Punchy II' of the 79th Fighter Group, 86th Fighter Squadron, 9th Air Force, on a desert airfield. (*via E. R. McDowell*).

Below: Open air maintenance work being carried out in the 79th Fighter Group dispersal area at Castel Benito, Tripolitania. (*IWM*).

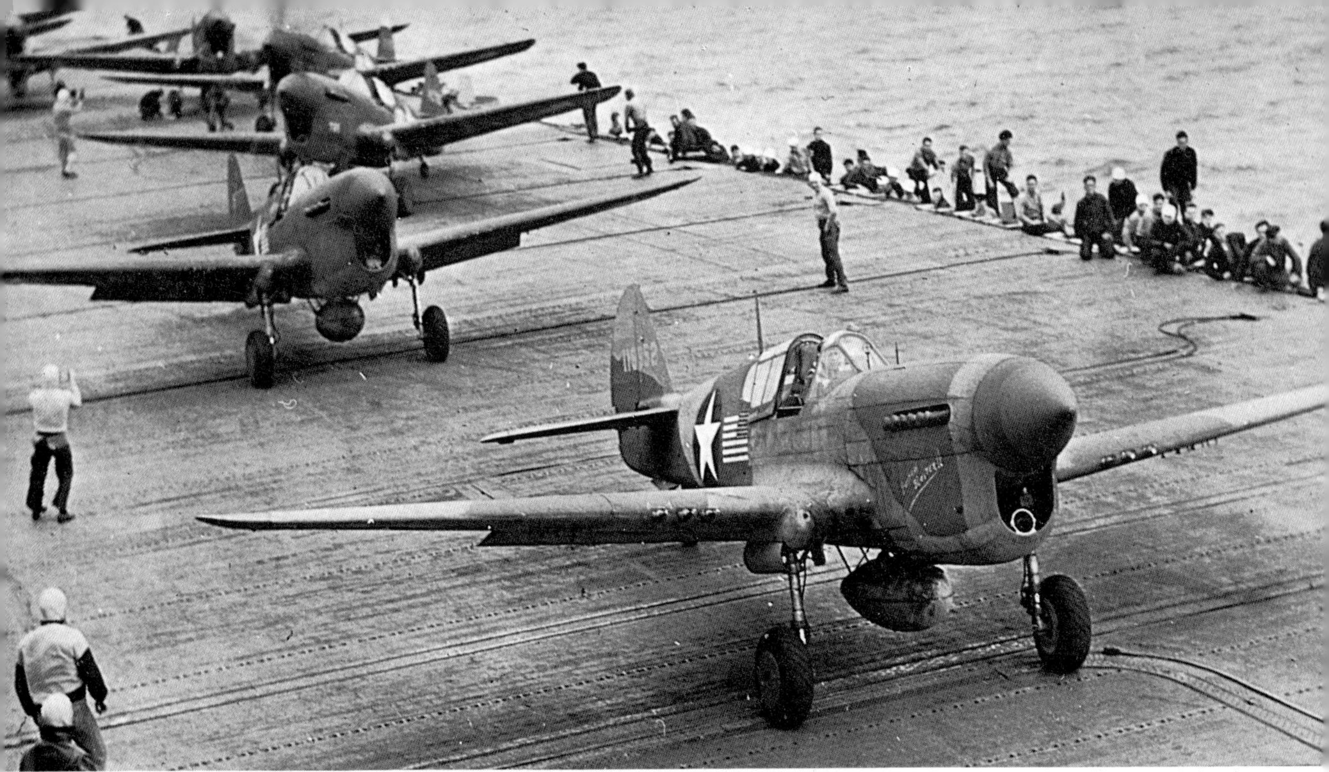

Above: P–40F's of the 325th Fighter Group lining up on the flight deck of the USS Ranger prior to taking off for Cazes airfield, Morocco, during the North African invasion, Operation 'Torch' 19th January, 1943. (*US Navy*).

Below: P–40F of the 33rd Fighter Group, 12th Air Force. Port Lyautey, French Morocco, Nov. 1942. Position and presentation of US Flag insignia varied and not all aircraft carried it on the under surface of the wings. Standard desert camouflage. (*IWM*).

Below: Warhawk taxying to dispersal area on an Algerian airfield, early 1943.

Armourers at work overhauling the ·5's of a P–40F of the 79th Fighter Group, 87th Fighter Squadron on Castel Benito airfield. Note cowl under wing waiting for the application of the unit insignia. (*USAF*).

P–40F flown by Major H. H. Green of the 325th 'Checkertails' Fighter Group, 15th Air Force, Italy. OD and Grey camouflage with yellow surround to the national insignia. Initials HHG on cowl design. (*via G. J. Letzter*).

P–40F used as a personal aircraft by either a Squadron or Group Commander in Italy. See colour illustration, note design in red on wheel disc. (*Fred C. Dickey*).

Above: Neat line-up of P–40F's probably of a training unit in the ZI. Nearest aircraft named 'Joyce', note white star on blue wheel disc. (*USAF*).

Above: Nice shot of a P–40E apparently in RAF green/brown camouflage. (*USAF*).
Below: P–40E of an unknown unit, white and red 'Sharkmouth' outlined in blue. (*USAF*).

Above: P–40K of the AAF Tactical Center Orlando Field, Florida, ZI. (*USAF*).

Right & below: 'Sharkmouthed' P–40N of the AAF Tactical Center, Orlando Field, Florida, ZI. Serial 323029, note fuselage stripes do not go all the way round the under surface. (*USAF*).

Very good clear detail photographs of a TP–40N, see colour illustration. (*USAF*).

Above: TP–40M of the AAF Tactical Center, Orlando Field, Florida, ZI. See colour illustration. 'Short Snorter', note dapple scheme. (*USAF*).
Below: P–40L of an unknown training unit, ZI. (*USAF*).

P–40R trainer (83rd P–40F re-engined). In natural metal with OD anti-glare panel, fin and rudder, red tip to spinner. (*Peter M. Bowers*).

P–40L in natural metal with OD anti-glare panel, X–896 and fin. Serial 211075. (*Peter M. Bowers*).

TP–40N in OD and grey scheme, white 708Y, serial 47068. (*Peter M. Bowers*)

TP–40N in natural metal with OD anti-glare panel and fin, serial 2105927. (*Roger F. Besecker*).

P–40N flown by Major B. Preston, OC of the 13th Fighter Group, see colour illustration. (*USAF via R. C. Jones*).

P–40N of the 369th Fighter Group, 398th Fighter Squadron, 3rd Air Force, ZI. (*USAF*).

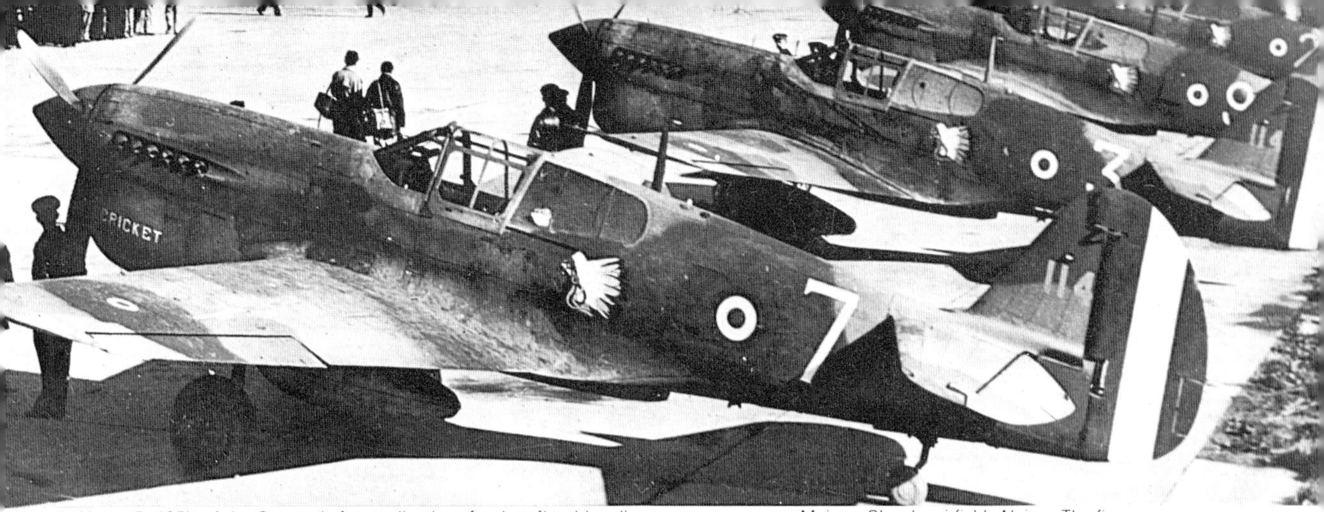

Above: P–40F's of the Groupe Lafayette lined up for the official handing over ceremony at Maison Blanche airfield, Algiers. The first three aircraft are of the 1st Escadrille and the fourth from the 2nd Escadrille. (*Etablissement Cinema des Armees*).

Left: P–40F of the 2nd Escadrille flown by Sgt. Chef Gisclon at Casablanca, January 1943. Note 'Stork' insignia under front cockpit, 6 in pale blue. (*via E. R. McDowell*).

Each Escadrille of the Groupe Lafayette used the same run of numbers, from 1 to 12 in the same style figures; 1st Esc. white, 2nd Esc. pale blue, 3rd Esc. red.

Below: P–40F and P–40L from the Meknes Fighter School flying over Morocco, March 1944. See colour illustrations. (*ECA*).

Below: P–40F of the Gunnery School, Sale, Morocco, March 1947. Note different style 4 on nose and fuselage. (*J. Cuny*).

Chinese Nationalist P–40F's flying escort to a formation of 14th Air Force B–24's. Note the first P–40 has white wing-tips and the others half white elevators, all but the lead P–40 with 'Sharkmouths'. (*USAF*).

P–40N of the Chinese Nationalist Air Force, Kangwan Field, 1946. (*Earl Reinert*).

P–40N modified as 2-seater, Kangwan Field, 1946. Chinese Nationalist Air Force. (*Earl Reinert*).

Right: P–40E in Japanese markings, probably captured in Java, old tank of a Buffalo in background. (*Peter M. Bowers*).

Below: P–40M of the Brazilian Air Force, see colour illustration. (*USAF via R. C. Jones*).

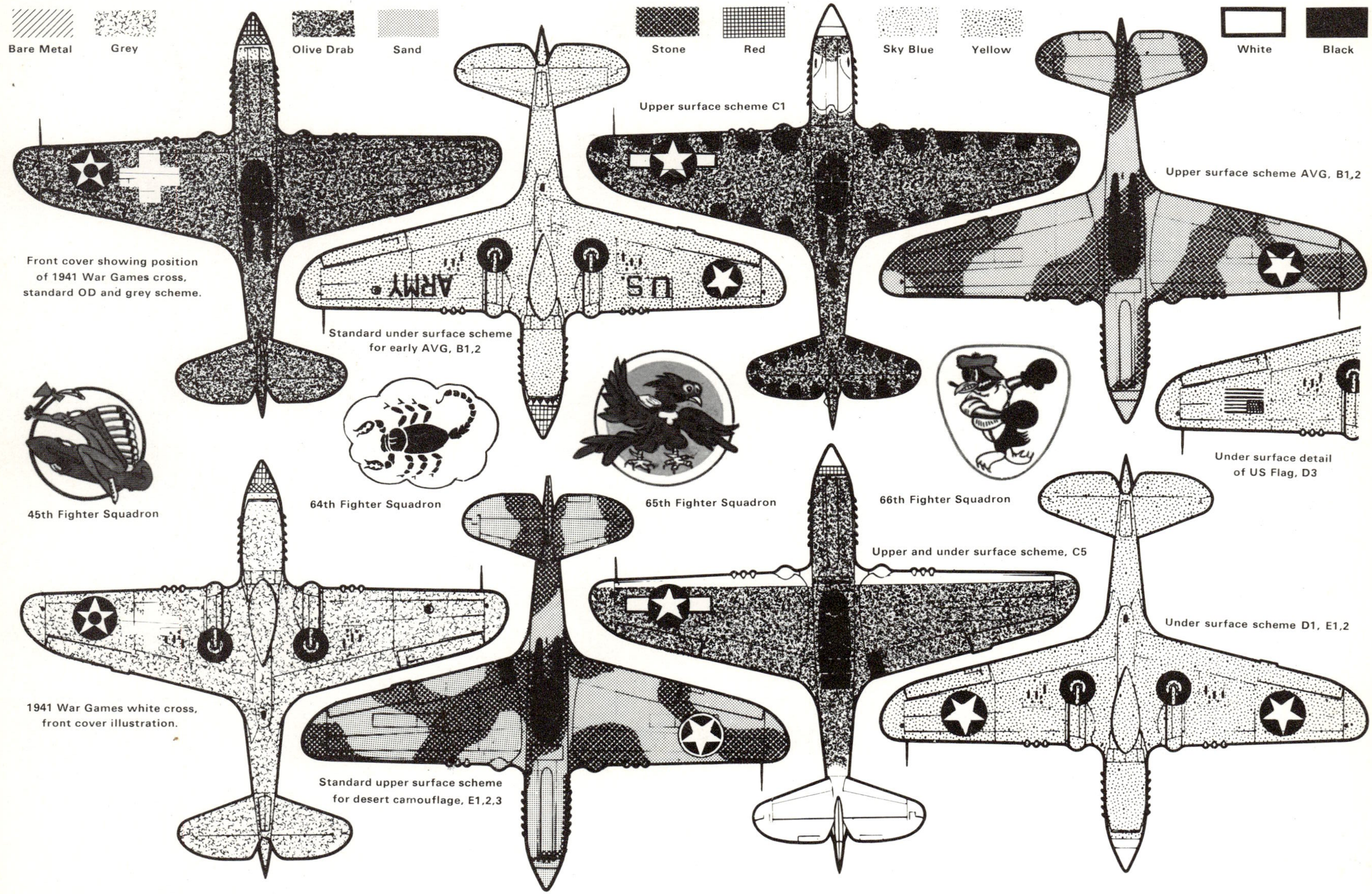
Bare Metal
Grey
Olive Drab
Sand
Stone
Red
Sky Blue
Yellow
White
Black
ARMY
US
Front cover showing position of 1941 War Games cross, standard OD and grey scheme.
Standard under surface scheme for early AVG, B1,2
Upper surface scheme C1
Upper surface scheme AVG, B1,2
Under surface detail of US Flag, D3
45th Fighter Squadron
64th Fighter Squadron
65th Fighter Squadron
66th Fighter Squadron
Upper and under surface scheme, C5
Under surface scheme D1, E1,2
1941 War Games white cross, front cover illustration.
Standard upper surface scheme for desert camouflage, E1,2,3